What Do They Become?

Written by Jared Kelner

Directed by Gerry Appel

2015 Venus/Adonis Theater Festival

The Robert Moss Theater at 440 Studios

440 Lafayette Street, 3rd Floor, New York, NY 10003

January 6, 2015 at 9:00 PM
January 7, 2015 at 6:15 PM
January 10, 2015 at 7:00 PM

What Do They Become? by Jared Kelner – copyright 2014
jared@jaredkelner.com – www.jaredkelner.com

Title: What Do They Become?
Publisher: The Infinite Mind Training Group
   (www.memory-trainers.com)
Playwright: Jared Kelner
   (www.jaredkelner.com)
Cover Art: CORSI DESIGN
   (corsi617@gmail.com)
ISBN-10: 0982655878
ISBN-13: 978-0-9826558-7-0

All rights reserved. No part of this book may be reproduced or transmitted in any form or by any means without written permission from the playwright, except for the inclusion of brief quotations in a review.

Copyright © 2014 by Jared Kelner

First Edition, 2014

Published in the United States of America

What Do They Become? by Jared Kelner – copyright 2014
jared@jaredkelner.com – www.jaredkelner.com

For Performance Inquires

Contact Jared Kelner

jared@jaredkelner.com

To watch a video of the

original cast performance, visit

www.jaredkelner.com/Pages/whatdotheybecome.aspx

What Do They Become? by Jared Kelner – copyright 2014
jared@jaredkelner.com – www.jaredkelner.com

What Do They Become? by Jared Kelner – copyright 2014
jared@jaredkelner.com – www.jaredkelner.com

A Note From The Playwright, Jared Kelner

This play was originally called "The Talk" and was quite meaningless. The characters were one dimensional, the circumstances were mundane and the message of the play was foggy at best. I'm not ashamed to admit that. I have no ego to protect. Writing, much like the craft of acting, is a constant journey and exploration to find truth. It took countless rewrites over 18 months to arrive at the play you are about to enjoy, and without thanking a few people, I would be doing a major disservice to those who helped and guided me along the way. I am forever in your debt.

Thank you to Eric Morace who read the first and second draft of this play and provided the honest and candid feedback that I needed to hear so I could reexamine what I was really trying to say. Without his unfiltered comments, *What Do They Become?* would not exist. You are a creative inspiration.

Thank you to my collaboration partner, co-teacher and never ending supporter, Gerry Appel. It's my sincere honor and privilege to know you, teach alongside you, and have you direct this play. You've helped us all discover the true meaning of *What Do They Become?*

Thank you to my friends and fellow cast mates, Marina, Sarah and Chris – you are all

What Do They Become? by Jared Kelner – copyright 2014
jared@jaredkelner.com – www.jaredkelner.com

uniquely amazing and talented. I cannot thank you enough for bringing life to the characters that have been living in my head for so long.

Thank you to my family: my son Coby for always letting me share my creativity with you even though I know you'd rather be solving a Fibonacci math equation; my daughter Tori for being the only one in the NJ Kelner-clan that appreciates the importance of creativity and imagination; and of course to my wife Debbie, for your patience, understanding and love. I know I often live in La La Land, but as Mayor of this imaginary world into which I frequently drift, I have many responsibilities. So please forgive me that I was wandering the streets of my imaginary world these last few months. The citizens of La La Land send their love and appreciation and wanted you to know that I'll return to you soon.

Finally, thank you to Franco and the Venus/Adonis Theater Festival Staff for accepting this play into the festival and providing the opportunity to share it with the world. You have all been incredibly supportive and that is greatly appreciated.

What Do They Become? by Jared Kelner – copyright 2014
jared@jaredkelner.com – www.jaredkelner.com

A Note From The Director, Gerry Appel

For the last four years, Jared Kelner, the playwright, and I have been co-teaching the adult acting classes at Playhouse Acting Academy. During that time, I had no idea that his talents also include playwriting. Jared first showed me his original script about a year ago. At the time, I was directing another original play, a comedy. I enjoy directing new works especially if the playwright is available. And, I was honored when Jared asked me to direct this show after it was selected for the Venus/Adonis Theater Festival.

Watching this talented cast, including the playwright, breathe life into these brand-new characters was a thrill. The new characters' relationships developed – beat by beat. And, now, the story that only existed in the playwright's head takes the stage. As with any developing work, I look forward to the audience's reaction. I don't like to explain the story line of a show I'm directing -- especially an original work. I don't believe the audience needs to be prepped for the production. That's the job of the actors and the script. Discovering an original play is exciting and allowing the story to unwind before your eyes on the stage is part of the joy of theater. I hope you enjoy this discovery half as much as I did.

What Do They Become? by Jared Kelner – copyright 2014
jared@jaredkelner.com – www.jaredkelner.com

What Do They Become? by Jared Kelner – copyright 2014
jared@jaredkelner.com – www.jaredkelner.com

CAST

JARED KELNER (Alan):

Jared studied acting in CA, NY, and NJ and has appeared professionally on stage, TV, and film. Favorite roles are Howard Corbett in *Rabbit Hole*, George Aaronow in *Glengarry Glen Ross*, and Arnold Epstein in *Biloxi Blues*. Jared will soon be seen in the independent film *Madeleine* directed by Ollie Verschoyle. Jared is honored to have his play brought to life by an incredible cast under the guidance of a talented and generous director. (jared@jaredkelner.com, www.jaredkelner.com)

MARINA VRAHNOS (Danielle):

Marina has had a passion for the stage since she was 5 years old. She attended the London Academy of Performing Arts where she grew up and went on to do Community Theater. Previous credits include *Equus*, *The Three Sisters*, *The Importance of Being Earnest*, and *Twelfth Night*. Since moving to the US, she has made several short films and produced and starred in *The Tiger* by Murray Schisgal. She has co-written and appeared in the Lawrence Play Fest for the past 4 years. One of her most recent roles for theatre was Eleanor in *The Lion in Winter*. Marina studies at the Playhouse Acting Academy in NJ, in which both her teachers are involved in with this play. Both Jared and Gerry have been such an inspiration for her. When not acting, Marina works as a massage therapist and models for life drawing classes. She hopes one day to do voice over work for children's books. (marinavrahnos@yahoo.com)

SARAH MACMILLAN (Amber/Samantha):

Sarah has had a wonderful time working with the very talented cast of *What Do They Become?* and is excited to play Samantha in her New York stage debut. She is grateful for the opportunity to explore this complex character under the direction of Gerry Appel. Sarah has studied at Playhouse Acting Academy in East Brunswick, NJ, and Weist-Barron Studios in New York City. Recent performances include *Honour* (Sophie), *A Hatful of Rain* (Celia), and *The Grapes of Wrath* (Narrator). Special thanks to the cast and her boyfriend, Chris O., for their support. (sarahharuko@gmail.com, www.backstage.com/sarahmacmillan)

CHRIS ROBERTSON (Vinnie/Johnny):

Chris is thrilled to be part of this production. Chris has been acting since the age of 6, studying the craft at ATC Studios in Clifton, NJ. He was recently seen at FringeNYC this past summer, starring in the original play *Skin in the Game*. Regional

Theater credits include *Midsummer Night's Dream* (Demetrius), *Romeo and Juliet* (Romeo), *Brighton Beach Memoirs* (Stanley), *Dead Man Walking* (Matt Poncelet), and many others. Chris is currently performing as a Knight at Medieval Times: Dinner and Tournament in Lyndhurst, NJ. Break legs everyone! (crobertson185@gmail.com, @chris7robertson, www.thechrisrobertson.com)

GERRY APPEL (Director):

Gerry is thrilled to be directing *What Do They Become?* with this awesome cast, including playwright/actor Jared Kelner. Past directing projects include *Twist of Faith* (an original play); *Gypsy*; *One Flew Over the Cuckoo's Nest*; *Dead Man's Cellphone*; *Little Shop of Horrors*; *Frankie and Johnny...*; *Lips Together, Teeth Apart*; *Mary, Mary*; *All in the Timing*, and several others. As director and teacher at the Playhouse Acting Academy (www.playhouseactingacademy.org) in East Brunswick, NJ, Gerry and his talented faculty encourage the creative development of actors. (njactingacademy@gmail.com)

CHRIS ORSI (Graphic Designer):

Cover poster created by Chris Orsi, from CORSI DESIGN. (corsi617@gmail.com)

What Do They Become? by Jared Kelner – copyright 2014
jared@jaredkelner.com – www.jaredkelner.com

What Do They Become? by Jared Kelner – copyright 2014
jared@jaredkelner.com – www.jaredkelner.com

What Do They Become?

Written by

Jared Kelner

SCENES

Scene 1: Alan and Danielle's house evening, just after a company party
Scene 2: A coffee shop, the next morning
Scene 3: Alan's office, later the same morning
Scene 4: Alan and Danielle's house, evening the same day
Scene 5: Amber and Vinnie's apartment, very late the same day
Scene 6: A coffee shop, the next morning
Scene 7: A park bench - around 6 PM the same day
Scene 8: Alan and Danielle's house, just before 7 PM the same day
Scene 9: A coffee shop, the next morning
Scene 10: Alan's office, around 9 AM the same day
Scene 11: A bus stop, around 10 AM the same day

Note: This play can be performed as a one-act play or a brief intermission can be taken between scenes 5 and 6.

.

What Do They Become?
Written by
Jared Kelner

CHARACTER DESCRIPTIONS

Alan: Early 40s, Danielle's husband. White Collar. Frustrated. Misguided. Vulnerable. Less than perfect. Conflicted.

Danielle: Early 40s, Alan's wife. Elegant. Sophisticated. Uptight. Prudish. Drinker. Lost. Lonely. Grasping at straws.

Amber/Samantha: Early 20s, Vinnie's girlfriend. Sensual. Seductive. Raw. Damaged. Manipulative. Cunning. Clever. Powerful. Empty. Co-Dependent.

Vinnie/Johnny: Early 20s, Amber's boyfriend. Intense. Powerful. Damaged. Cunning. Threatening. Determined. Focused. Abused. Empty. Alone. Angry.

What Do They Become? by Jared Kelner – copyright 2014
jared@jaredkelner.com – www.jaredkelner.com

What Do They Become?

Written by

Jared Kelner

SET LAYOUT & DESIGN

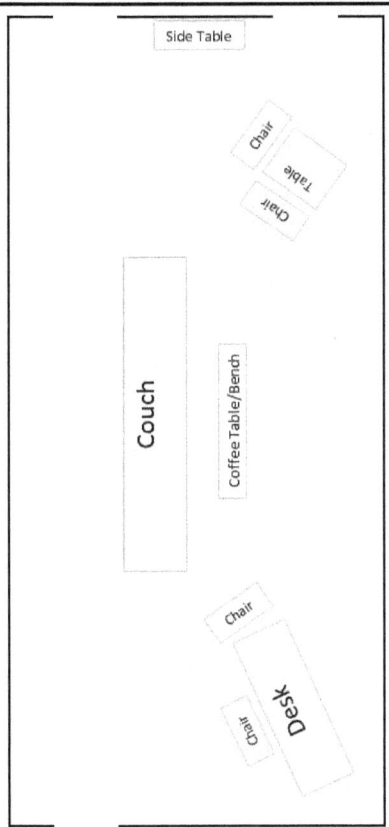

What Do They Become? by Jared Kelner – copyright 2014
jared@jaredkelner.com – www.jaredkelner.com

What Do They Become? by Jared Kelner – copyright 2014
jared@jaredkelner.com – www.jaredkelner.com

What Do They Become?

Written by

Jared Kelner

Scene 1: (Alan and Danielle's house, evening, just after a company party) Alan enters upstage left and turns on the light and is immediately followed by Danielle. Center stage is a couch with a coffee table in front of it (the coffee table doubles for the bench in scene 5). There is a blanket and 2 throw pillows on the couch. Downstage left is the kitchen with a small table with 2 chairs; 1 upstage right and 1 upstage left. The door to the bedroom is downstage left. Downstage right is a desk with a chair just upstage of it and a second chair stage left of the desk. The house is simple without clutter. Prior to entering, we hear Alan and Danielle arguing but cannot make out exactly what they are saying.

DANIELLE. Who is she, Alan? Don't make me ask you again.
ALAN. Nobody. Just someone from work.
DANIELLE. What did you do?

What Do They Become? by Jared Kelner – copyright 2014
jared@jaredkelner.com – www.jaredkelner.com

ALAN. I told you. We didn't do anything.

DANIELLE. Alan, please respect me enough to not lie as you are running away from me.

ALAN. I am not lying this time.

DANIELLE. Who is she?

ALAN. She works in the office. She's nobody.

DANIELLE. Do you hate me that much that you would risk our marriage, especially now, for someone who's nobody?

ALAN. Danielle, don't blow this out of proportion. I do not hate you. I love you.

DANIELLE. Then explain it to me, Alan. If she's nobody and you love me, why?

ALAN. Why what?

DANIELLE. Do you mean to torture me? Haven't you the guts to admit it?

ALAN. Now you're just being dramatic.

DANIELLE. Alan! Tell me who she is and why you were in the bathroom together at that pathetic party and don't you dare lie.

ALAN. Sam.

DANIELLE. Sam?

ALAN. Sam. Samantha.

What Do They Become? by Jared Kelner – copyright 2014
jared@jaredkelner.com – www.jaredkelner.com

DANIELLE. Who is Sam, Samantha, Alan?

ALAN. She works in the office. She's new.

DANIELLE. New to you?

ALAN. She's new at the office.

DANIELLE. Yes, I heard you, but I asked you if she was new to you or is she just new to the office?

ALAN. Yes.

DANIELLE. Yes, what, Alan? Spit it out.

ALAN. You're drunk again. Go to bed and we'll talk in the morning.

DANIELLE. I am not drunk, Alan. You've seen me drunk before. Do I look drunk to you?

ALAN. Yes.

DANIELLE. Coward. You just don't want to talk about the failure that is our marriage.

ALAN. Don't say that, Danielle. Not with the baby coming.

DANIELLE. Coward.

ALAN. I'm going to bed.

DANIELLE. You will not weasel out of this, Alan. Be a man. I beg you. Be the man who stood by me through my problems. Be the man who said yes to adopt a baby with me after all these years.

What Do They Become? by Jared Kelner – copyright 2014
jared@jaredkelner.com – www.jaredkelner.com

ALAN. Foster, not adopt, Danielle. Foster.

DANIELLE. Semantics, Alan. We are going to be parents.

ALAN. I know that.

DANIELLE. So, why now?

ALAN. Ninety-four.

DANIELLE. What does ninety-four mean?

ALAN. Ninety-four days since the last time we had sex.

DANIELLE. You're keeping track? You're counting days? What are you, a teenager?

ALAN. I'm a man, Danielle, with needs and you've shut down. The truth is you don't love me and you haven't really loved me in years.

DANIELLE. Alan, just because we have not made love in a while-

ALAN. Ninety-four days.

DANIELLE. I'm choosing to ignore that. That is ridiculous. Just because we have not made love in however long it's been has nothing to do with my love for you and...Wait. You sneaky bastard. This is not about me or ninety-four days, Alan. This is about you. You and Samantha and the bathroom and you better come clean.

ALAN. What do you want me to tell you?

DANIELLE. The truth.

What Do They Become? by Jared Kelner – copyright 2014
jared@jaredkelner.com – www.jaredkelner.com

ALAN. She smiles when I say "Good morning." She laughs at my jokes.

DANIELLE. Would you like me to laugh at your jokes, Alan?

ALAN. Don't patronize me.

DANIELLE. Then tell me the truth. Let's not forget why we are talking right now. You made a choice. The wrong choice...again. You chose to make ninety-four days mean so much that you lost sight of what truly matters. You lost sight of me. You lost sight of wanting to be a father. That breaks my heart, Alan.

ALAN. I kissed her.

DANIELLE. I know you did. You still have her lipstick on your cheek.

ALAN. I love you.

DANIELLE. Don't do that.

ALAN. What about the baby?

DANIELLE. One thing at a time, Alan.

ALAN. You're not backing out, Danielle. Not after all we've been through to get this child.

DANIELLE. You should have thought about that before you went into the bathroom.

ALAN. But we have to let them know.

What Do They Become? by Jared Kelner – copyright 2014
jared@jaredkelner.com – www.jaredkelner.com

DANIELLE. One thing at a time.

ALAN. Couch?

DANIELLE. Yes.

ALAN. It will never happen again.

DANIELLE. I've heard that before. Now's not the time to make promises you can't keep.

ALAN. I love you.

DANIELLE. Goodnight, Alan.

(Danielle exits to their bedroom. Lights out)

Scene 2: (A coffee shop, the next morning) The lights come up downstage left on the coffee shop. The kitchen table and chairs double for the coffee shop sidewalk table. The change of location is communicated through lighting. The set pieces do not need to be moved. Samantha is standing outside the coffee shop next to the table and makes a call on her cellphone to her boyfriend. While Samantha is on the phone, Danielle is offstage left "inside" the coffee shop.

AMBER. (Leaving a voice mail on the phone) Hey, it's me. I guess you're still sleeping. Look, I know today is going to be hard for you like it is every year, but I want you to know that you are loved and what we do, that's how we keep his memory alive. Please try to have an easy day today. OK, I gotta go. I'll see you tonight. I love you, baby. (As Amber finishes leaving her voice mail, Danielle exits the coffee shop through the open doorway. She wears dark sunglasses and has a headache from drinking last night. Amber hangs up the phone, becomes Samantha, turns and bumps into Danielle.)

SAMANTHA. Oh. Excuse me. I'm sorry.

DANIELLE. It's ok.

SAMANTHA. Wait. You look familiar. Do I know you?

DANIELLE. (Recognizing Samantha) No. I don't believe so.

SAMANTHA. No. I'm sure we've met. Where do you work out?

DANIELLE. I don't.

SAMANTHA. Really? Come on, we've met somewhere.

DANIELLE. We do not know each other.

SAMANTHA. OK, if you say so. I'm Sam, Samantha, by the way.

DANIELLE. (Under her breath) I know who you are.

SAMANTHA. What?

DANIELLE. Nothing.

What Do They Become? by Jared Kelner – copyright 2014
jared@jaredkelner.com – www.jaredkelner.com

SAMANTHA. No. Wait. Did you just say you know who I am?

DANIELLE. I know who you are.

SAMANTHA. I knew we met. What's your name again?

DANIELLE. I did not give you my name.

SAMANTHA. I know you didn't just now, but I mean before, when you did give me your name. I'm so bad with names. My boyfriend Johnny is really good with names. He's a cop and all. Not one of those fat donut cops. He's all hot and badass and shit. I mean, what's your name again?

DANIELLE. It's not again. I did not give you my name. You do not know my name, but I know you. And now I know more about you.

SAMANTHA. Wait. What?

DANIELLE. (Taking off her sunglasses) Look at me.

SAMANTHA. I'm looking at you.

DANIELLE. Who am I?

SAMANTHA. That's what I'm asking you. Who are you?

DANIELLE. Look at me.

SAMANTHA. I'm looking.

DANIELLE. Do you see me Sam, Samantha?

SAMANTHA. Yeah, I see you and all, but...wait. Oh...I know who you are.

DANIELLE. You know who I am?

SAMANTHA. Yeah.

DANIELLE. Who am I, Sam, Samantha?

SAMANTHA. You're um...

DANIELLE. Spit it out, Sam, Samantha.

SAMANTHA. You're Alan's wife, right?

DANIELLE. I'm Alan's wife, Sam, Samantha.

SAMANTHA. Why do you keep saying that?

DANIELLE. Saying what, Sam, Samantha?

SAMANTHA. My name, twice. It's freaking me out.

DANIELLE. Well, Sam, Samantha, the last thing I want to do is make you uncomfortable. I mean, gosh, where are my manners?

SAMANTHA. Look. I get it. I do. Your husband fucked up. But you're attacking the wrong person.

DANIELLE. Is that so? Who should I be attacking? Myself?

SAMANTHA. How about Alan, lady?

DANIELLE. Excuse me?

SAMANTHA. Well what the fuck do you want me to call you? If you got a name, then tell me and I'll use it. But don't you come off snapping at me, without first telling me your name. Acting all high and mighty and shit. My man wasn't in the bathroom with another woman. I know how to please my man, lady.

DANIELLE. It's Danielle. Enough with the lady, Sam, Samantha.

SAMANTHA. OK, Dan, Danielle. Come on! You can't be serious now! He didn't tell me he was married. It's not my fault. He makes me laugh.

DANIELLE. That's my husband.

SAMANTHA. I know that now. I mean I knew that the moment we walked out of the bathroom and I saw you and then saw him.

DANIELLE. What about Johnny? Does he know you're a cheater?

SAMANTHA. There you go again, Danielle. Open your eyes. It's not my fault and Johnny doesn't care. He's just my boyfriend.

DANIELLE. (Sits down at the table) Why?

SAMANTHA. Why what?

DANIELLE. Why does he make you laugh?

SAMANTHA. He's funny.

DANIELLE. Alan?

SAMANTHA. Yes, Alan. You don't see it?

DANIELLE. No. Not anymore.

SAMANTHA. (Sits down at the table) That's a shame, cause he is, funny I mean.

DANIELLE. He's never funny with me.

SAMANTHA. Why?

DANIELLE. I don't want to answer that.

SAMANTHA. Then you know. So you see, it's not my fault.

DANIELLE. I'm sorry, Sam, Samantha...Forgive me. Samantha.

SAMANTHA. Just call me Sam.

DANIELLE. Is that what Alan calls you?

SAMANTHA. Danielle!

DANIELLE. Damn it...Tell me, please.

SAMANTHA. No way. That's for you to discuss with your husband.

DANIELLE. Oh, we've discussed. I just need to know if what was discussed is any more disgusting than what I know.

SAMANTHA. Disgusting? What did he tell you?

DANIELLE. That he kissed you.

SAMANTHA. And?

DANIELLE. That's not enough?

SAMANTHA. You said it was disgusting.

What Do They Become? by Jared Kelner – copyright 2014
jared@jaredkelner.com – www.jaredkelner.com

DANIELLE. It is.

SAMANTHA. No, Danielle. A kiss is not disgusting. A kiss is nothing.

DANIELLE. A kiss is not nothing when he's done it before.

SAMANTHA. Oh. Well there is a lot more we could have done in the bathroom that would've been disgusting.

DANIELLE. And what would that be?

SAMANTHA. That would be nothing.

DANIELLE. Yeah, well...what kind of kiss was it?

SAMANTHA. Are you serious? Are you some kind of freak that you need to know if I put my tongue in your husband's mouth?

DANIELLE. I need to hear it.

SAMANTHA. Ask your husband.

DANIELLE. I can't.

SAMANTHA. Oh Danielle, it was just a kiss. This is so sad. I can see you love him, so why is he kissing me? Why is he not kissing you?

DANIELLE. Because...well...because I'm old and fat and I'm not young like you.

SAMANTHA. Danielle. You're beautiful and you are not fat. If I look as good as you look when I'm your age, I'd think I was hot.

What Do They Become? by Jared Kelner – copyright 2014
jared@jaredkelner.com – www.jaredkelner.com

DANIELLE. You think I'm beautiful?

SAMANTHA. Yes, you are a beautiful woman. So what's the deal? Why did your husband take me into the bathroom?

DANIELLE. I'm embarrassed to say it.

SAMANTHA. Look. I know we just met, but I like you. You make me want to hug you. Just talk to me like we're girlfriends.

DANIELLE. Girlfriends? You kissed my husband. I should be angry at you.

SAMANTHA. But you're not, are you?

DANIELLE. No, I'm not angry at you. Jealous maybe, but not angry.

SAMANTHA. So then tell me. What's going on?

DANIELLE. Ninety-four. No, actually, it's ninety-five now.

SAMANTHA. What does that mean?

DANIELLE. Ninety-five days since, you know?

SAMANTHA. No. What's ninety-five days?

DANIELLE. Since Alan and I...you know. The last time we...

SAMANTHA. GET THE FUCK OUT OF HERE!!!!!

DANIELLE. SSSHHHH!!!!

SAMANTHA. Are you kidding me? What is your problem?

DANIELLE. I told you. I'm fat.

What Do They Become? by Jared Kelner – copyright 2014
jared@jaredkelner.com – www.jaredkelner.com

SAMANTHA. You stupid bitch. You're not fat. What is the matter with you? How can you deprive your husband for three months? How can you deprive yourself? Holy crap. My brain is exploding just trying to wrap my head around this shit.

DANIELLE. I'm just never in the mood.

SAMANTHA. But you do it anyway, cause you love him.

DANIELLE. But, I don't. I mean, I do love him, but I don't just do it anyway.

SAMANTHA. So that's it. This is so easy to fix. You just need to spice things up. You gotta surprise him. Like bring toys into bed. Or bring a hot young chick like me into bed with you both.

DANIELLE. What?

SAMANTHA. Come on, Danielle. Please tell me you've had a threesome.

DANIELLE. I will not. I have never.

SAMANTHA. What a prude.

DANIELLE. And what's your point?

SAMANTHA. Look, your man pulls me into the bathroom and kisses me. And yes, it was one of "those" kisses. So, why does he do it?

DANIELLE. Because you laugh at his jokes.

What Do They Become? by Jared Kelner – copyright 2014
jared@jaredkelner.com – www.jaredkelner.com

SAMANTHA. No, Danielle. Why does he kiss me?

DANIELLE. Because...

SAMANTHA. Because, what?

DANIELLE. Because I drink too much sometimes.

SAMANTHA. And?

DANIELLE. Because I don't kiss him.

SAMANTHA. And there we have it. Hala-fucking-luyah.

DANIELLE. So what do I do now?

SAMANTHA. You kiss that motherfucker like you've never kissed him before.

DANIELLE. Just out of the blue. Just kiss him?

SAMANTHA. Yes.

DANIELLE. And then what?

SAMANTHA. Then you slap his ass. You pinch his nipples. You bite his lip til he bleeds. You take your husband back. What? What's that look for?

DANIELLE. You're hot, Samantha.

SAMANTHA. Excuse me?

DANIELLE. I'm sorry. I'm flushed right now. Maybe I'm hungover. I don't know, but you're hot. You're right, but you're hot too. You're making me have thoughts I don't understand.

SAMANTHA. You feeling dirty?

What Do They Become? by Jared Kelner – copyright 2014
jared@jaredkelner.com – www.jaredkelner.com

DANIELLE. Maybe.

SAMANTHA. What kind of thoughts are you having?

DANIELLE. Inappropriate ones.

SAMANTHA. That's what I'm talking about, Danielle. You want to kiss me?

DANIELLE. No. I don't know. Maybe.

SAMANTHA. Well do you?

DANIELLE. Yes.

SAMANTHA. Well, too bad. You don't get to kiss me. You take that cougar inside you now and you pounce on Alan.

DANIELLE. But I don't know how to pounce.

SAMANTHA. You don't know how to pounce?

DANIELLE. Do you know how to pounce?

SAMANTHA. Oh, honey, I can pounce.

DANIELLE. Then you have to help me. You need to be there.

SAMANTHA. Danielle, let's not get carried away.

DANIELLE. I know this is going to sound crazy, but what do you think he'll say if you came over tomorrow night and we had one of those threesomes you said are amazing?

SAMANTHA. I never said they were amazing.

DANIELLE. But they are, aren't they?

SAMANTHA. They are amazing, but you can never undo a threesome.

DANIELLE. I don't care.

SAMANTHA. You have no idea what you are talking about.

DANIELLE. You're right, but it's the only way.

SAMANTHA. You know that you and Alan are totally fucked up, right?

DANIELLE. Yeah, I know it, but I don't care anymore. (Danielle reaches into her purse and pulls out a pen. Danielle writes her address on a napkin and pushes it over to Samantha).

SAMANTHA. What's this?

DANIELLE. My address and you're coming over tomorrow night, you hear me?

SAMANTHA. You really want to do this?

DANIELLE. Yes.

SAMANTHA. And you want to do this with me, even after Alan kissed me?

DANIELLE. It's because Alan kissed you. I don't care if it doesn't make sense. Something has to change.

SAMANTHA. OK, then. I'll do it. I'll tell Johnny I've got to work late and I'll come over tomorrow around seven.

DANIELLE. Yes.

SAMANTHA. You sure?

DANIELLE. It needs to be done.

SAMANTHA. OK. I gotta get to work now.

DANIELLE. Please do not say anything to Alan.

SAMANTHA. I won't.

DANIELLE. Thank you. I'll see you tomorrow.

SAMANTHA. See you tomorrow.

(Samantha leaves. Lights out)

Scene 3: (Alan's office, later the same morning) The lights come up stage right on the office. Alan sits at his desk. On the desk is a full pen/pencil holder, a notebook, some papers, and an apple. Alan is on the phone finishing a conversation as Samantha enters and plops herself down in the chair, ignoring the fact that Alan is conducting business.

ALAN. (Into the phone) I understand, Mike. I know budgets are tight. The whole "do more with less" nonsense is killing me. We lost David last week to some start-up. Yes, David. It's a big loss. So, about the proposal, hear me out. I can drop the price by 25%, but you have to cut three orders and make them all less than $50K so it flies under the radar. Can we make it work, like old times? Yeah? Awesome! That's great, Mike. Thank you. I owe you one, again. I'll email you the quote in an hour. OK. Yeah, I will. I'll let her know you say hi. Alright. Bye. (Alan hangs up the phone)

SAMANTHA. Look at you, Mr. Sales Manager, closing business and shit. You go, Alan. You book that shit.

ALAN. Sam, you can't just barge in here and plop yourself down when I'm on the phone.

SAMANTHA. I didn't barge, Alan. Your door was open. And I didn't plop. That sounds so gross anyway. All I did was come in and sit down. My god, you're wound tight today. Relax. Be happy. You just closed some business. That's a good thing right?

ALAN. Yes. It's a good thing.

SAMANTHA. Then be happy, Alan. I'm happy. I'm happy for you. See, look at me smile all big and shit for you.

ALAN. Samantha, come on. You can't curse at the office. It's not professional.

SAMANTHA. Get the fuck out of here.

ALAN. I'm serious. You have to act professionally.

SAMANTHA. Is that what you want from me, to be a professional?

ALAN. All I'm saying is just watch the words you use when you're at work. People will take you seriously if you talk more, adult-like.

SAMANTHA. Are you calling me a child, Alan?

ALAN. No, of course not. I'm just saying, don't curse at work. That's all.

SAMANTHA. OK, boss. No more cursing at work. You got it. The potty mouth has been locked up.

ALAN. Thank you.

SAMANTHA. You're welcome. So, about the other night.

ALAN. Let's not do this now.

SAMANTHA. You want to do it later? Maybe like, tomorrow night?

ALAN. No. What about tomorrow night?

SAMANTHA. Nothing.

ALAN. I meant, I just don't want to talk about it here, now.

SAMANTHA. OK, it's cool. No big deal. So, what about the promotion and shit? Oh, crap. I'm sorry. Potty mouth. It's locked up again. Seriously though, you said that since David is gone that I can have the job, right?

What Do They Become? by Jared Kelner – copyright 2014
jared@jaredkelner.com – www.jaredkelner.com

ALAN. Well. I mean, we have to backfill his role, yes, but there's a process.

SAMANTHA. OK. How do I get processed?

ALAN. No. What I mean is there's an interview process.

SAMANTHA. Wait, what? Interview? You didn't say anything about an interview at the party, Alan. You said that the job was practically mine.

ALAN. Practically speaking, it's more complicated than that.

SAMANTHA. OK. I can be mature about this. What do I have to do to get the job? Should we go into the bathroom again?

ALAN. Come on. You know I can't do that again. Maybe you shouldn't be in my office right now.

SAMANTHA. Relax. You're wound so tight. What's the matter? You all backed up?

ALAN. What?

SAMANTHA. You're so tense. It's been a while, huh? You're all serious like you haven't gotten any in like three months or something.

ALAN. What did you say?

SAMANTHA. I'm just playing with you. Look, let's get back to my career ok?

What Do They Become? by Jared Kelner – copyright 2014
jared@jaredkelner.com – www.jaredkelner.com

ALAN. Yeah, ok.

SAMANTHA. So, what do I have to do to get the job?

ALAN. Well, you interview for it.

SAMANTHA. Come on, Alan. I can do this sales shit. You know that, right?

ALAN. I mean, I know you're a hard worker, but if you want me to talk seriously now, I will.

SAMANTHA. Of course, Alan. I want you to be honest with me, always.

ALAN. OK. Well, you work hard, but you come across...young sometimes.

SAMANTHA. I think it's probably because I am young, Alan. I just turned twenty. So I act my age. Is that so bad?

ALAN. Well, outside the office, no. But at work, people expect you to act more mature.

SAMANTHA. Mature like you?

ALAN. I guess.

SAMANTHA. Making good decisions like you, right, Alan?

ALAN. I try.

SAMANTHA. How hard do you try?

ALAN. I try.

SAMANTHA. OK, so I'll act more mature like you and I'll make big girl decisions like you. Not that you're a girl. You know what I mean. I'll make big boy decisions, but like a girl, or like a woman.

ALAN. Yes, like a woman.

SAMANTHA. OK, and then what?

ALAN. Well, then there's the interview.

SAMANTHA. OK. So let's do the interview.

ALAN. Now?

SAMANTHA. Sure, why not now? You're here. I'm here. Interview me.

ALAN. OK. Why do you want the job?

SAMANTHA. Well, sir, I've learned so much from you over the last few months that I know I'm ready to do more for you and for the company, make more of an impact than I can today.

ALAN. Nice.

SAMANTHA. Thank you, sir. You see, I haven't had it easy like the others here and I have to think about my future. If you were to take a chance on me, you'd help me save money for maybe a family one day.

ALAN. Holy shit, Sam.

SAMANTHA. Language, Alan.

ALAN. Sorry.

What Do They Become? by Jared Kelner – copyright 2014
jared@jaredkelner.com – www.jaredkelner.com

SAMANTHA. Also, I'm a people person. People love me. I can sell anything to anyone and I'm ready to use everything at my disposal to get what I want.

ALAN. Is that so?

SAMANTHA. Yes, sir.

ALAN. OK, then. Sell me this apple.

SAMANTHA. OK. (She takes the apple) Hi there.

ALAN. Hi.

SAMANTHA. It's nice out today, isn't it?

ALAN. Yeah. Nice breeze.

SAMANTHA. I know, right. I love this time of year. It makes me think of my childhood.

ALAN. Really?

SAMANTHA. Yeah. I remember feeling a breeze like this one day when I was with my daddy and he took me to an orchard. He held my hand and I got to carry the basket.

ALAN. What basket?

SAMANTHA. The basket for the apples of course. Daddy loved holding my hand and telling me that one day I was going to grow up and become a beautiful young lady.

ALAN. He sounds like a wonderful man.

SAMANTHA. I know, right. Daddy was strong and handsome and funny. He always made me laugh. So one day, we went apple picking at the orchard. Daddy picked me up and held me high above his head and then spun me around so I could sit on his shoulders. I was so high off the ground, but I felt safe with him, like he was going to protect me forever.

ALAN. You are lucky to have a father who loved you like that.

SAMANTHA. Aw. That's sweet. (Starting her seduction) So anyway, we walked through the orchard and I picked the biggest, reddest, juiciest apples right off the trees and put them in my basket. Then we sat down under one of the trees in the shade. Daddy let me pick which apple we were going to share and then he washed it off with some water and then he said, "You first, Sammie. You take a big, juicy bite and tell me how sweet it tastes."

ALAN. And how did it taste?

SAMANTHA. So good. So sweet. My small, white, innocent teeth pierced the skin and when they sank deep into the apple, juice just exploded all over my face and I swallowed the sweet, sweet apple. And it was good.

ALAN. How good was it?

SAMANTHA. So good.

ALAN. I need to buy an apple.

SAMANTHA. No.

ALAN. Why not?

SAMANTHA. Cause I only have this one apple and I was going to eat it.

ALAN. But I want to eat the apple.

SAMANTHA. You want to eat the apple?

ALAN. I want to eat the apple.

SAMANTHA. You want to eat my apple.

ALAN. Yes, I want to eat your apple.

SAMANTHA. How much is my apple worth to you?

ALAN. Whatever you want.

SAMANTHA. How about $20 for just one bite of my sweet, juicy apple.

ALAN. (He takes a $20 bill from his wallet and places it on the desk) Sure, here. One bite. $20.

SAMANTHA. (She leaves the money on the desk) Open your mouth. Wider. Tilt your head back. Good boy. Close your eyes.

ALAN. I want your apple.

SAMANTHA. Here you go. Slowly. Don't rush. Gently bite my apple.

ALAN. (He takes a bite) Mmmmmmmmm.

SAMANTHA. Oh that's so yummy, right?

What Do They Become? by Jared Kelner – copyright 2014
jared@jaredkelner.com – www.jaredkelner.com

ALAN. I want more.

SAMANTHA. Tomorrow.

ALAN. Tomorrow?

SAMANTHA. Tomorrow. I'll give you more of my apple tomorrow. Bring your wallet. My apples are very expensive.

ALAN. OK.

SAMANTHA. (Snapping out of the seduction) So, Alan, can I keep the $20? I did pretty good right? You can think about it, but I know I can knock the shit out of this job. Make the right decision. (Samantha takes the $20 and eats the apple as she leaves)

ALAN. Fuck me!

(Lights out)

Scene 4: (Alan and Danielle's house, evening the same day) The lights come up full again on the entire house. Danielle is seated at the kitchen table, lost in time. She has finished eating the dinner she prepared for her and Alan. Alan's plate has cold food on it. There is a half-empty bottle of white wine on the table; Danielle's glass of wine is nearly empty, too. Alan enters through the upstage left door, softly closes it behind him, and crosses downstage right of Danielle. He is holding his briefcase.

ALAN. I'm home.

DANIELLE. Yes, I can see. You are later than I expected.

ALAN. I've been sitting in the car for a while. I wasn't sure if I was allowed to come in.

DANIELLE. This is still your home, Alan.

ALAN. I know, but...I mean...since, you know.

DANIELLE. I see.

ALAN. May I stay?

DANIELLE. This is still your home, Alan.

ALAN. Thank you, Danielle. Is that...did you make dinner...for me?

DANIELLE. I made dinner. Mine is gone. Yours is cold by now.

ALAN. Cold is fine.

DANIELLE. Then put your stuff down and come sit.

ALAN. Would that be all right?

DANIELLE. Yes.

ALAN. (Alan hangs his coat up on the hook by the door, puts his wallet, keys and computer bag on the side table by the door, crosses to the table and sits) This looks wonderful.

DANIELLE. Thank you.

ALAN. May I ask how your day was today?

DANIELLE. You may.

ALAN. How was your day?

DANIELLE. Like any other day.

ALAN. I'm glad to hear that. I was thinking all day that maybe today for you, would be very different from any other day.

DANIELLE. Well, it wasn't. Today was just like every day. I got up. I showered. I got dressed. I put my makeup on. I did my hair and I went to get coffee.

ALAN. That does sound like every other day.

DANIELLE. Yes.

ALAN. What did you do after the coffee shop?

DANIELLE. Why are you asking me about the coffee shop?

ALAN. I'm not. I'm sorry. I was asking what you did after the coffee shop.

DANIELLE. Does it matter, Alan? Does it matter what happened after the coffee shop?

ALAN. No, I suppose not. Sorry.

DANIELLE. So, how was your day?

What Do They Become? by Jared Kelner – copyright 2014
jared@jaredkelner.com – www.jaredkelner.com

ALAN. My day? Oh, my day was ok, good I guess. I mean, not good like there's nothing going on in my head every three seconds, but I mean work itself was good, business-wise.

DANIELLE. Oh, is that right? Did you have a good business day?

ALAN. Yeah. It was a good business day. I talked to Mike.

DANIELLE. Did you?

ALAN. Yeah.

DANIELLE. But the judge said you're not permitted to be in contact with him anymore.

ALAN. I know, but I had to.

DANIELLE. Is that right, Alan? You had to?

ALAN. What do you want me to say? I have to earn a living if we're going to adopt a baby.

DANIELLE. Foster, Alan. Now I'm correcting you.

ALAN. Danielle, they told us how these things work. You foster and then sometimes you adopt.

DANIELLE. Please do not lecture me.

ALAN. I'm not lecturing....You're right. I'm sorry. I shouldn't have called Mike.

DANIELLE. And what else happened at the office today... business-wise?

What Do They Become? by Jared Kelner – copyright 2014
jared@jaredkelner.com – www.jaredkelner.com

ALAN. What do you mean?

DANIELLE. What do you suppose I mean?

ALAN. Well, I think you're asking me if I saw her today.

DANIELLE. Am I?

ALAN. Well, aren't you?

DANIELLE. Perhaps. I assumed you saw...her...today, since she does work in your office, Alan.

ALAN. Yes, she does. She does work in the office.

DANIELLE. So then, yes?

ALAN. Um, yeah. Yes, I saw her today. She came into my office.

DANIELLE. Oh, well that's different, Alan. Seeing her AT the office and seeing her IN your office are two very different things. Was it wise of you to see her IN your office today of all days?

ALAN. No. I probably should not have seen her in my office.

DANIELLE. You're probably right, Alan. You should trust your instincts.

ALAN. Yes, I should.

DANIELLE. And did you kiss her today in your office, Alan.

ALAN. No. I'm not going to kiss her in my office.

DANIELLE. Oh, but you would kiss her outside of your office, like in a bathroom?

ALAN. No, Danielle, that's not what I'm saying. You're putting words in my mouth.

DANIELLE. You don't like things put in your mouth, Alan?

ALAN. What?

DANIELLE. Your mouth, Alan. I'm asking you if you do or do not like things to be put into your mouth.

ALAN. Nothing is in my mouth. She didn't put anything in my mouth.

DANIELLE. What are you talking about?

ALAN. Nothing. You're confusing me. I'm just saying nothing is in my mouth.

DANIELLE. OK. Nothing is in your mouth. I can see that. That's a good thing, because when you put things into your mouth that should not be put into your mouth, Alan, we end up where we are.

ALAN. And where are we, Danielle?

DANIELLE. Well, we're at the dinner table, Alan, with cold food and cheap wine.

ALAN. You know what I mean. I can't keep dancing around it like this. I'm never going to win a verbal battle with you.

What Do They Become? by Jared Kelner – copyright 2014
jared@jaredkelner.com – www.jaredkelner.com

DANIELLE. Is that what you want? To win a battle over me?

ALAN. No. That's what I mean. You twist my words and make me sound like a fool.

DANIELLE. Well Alan, you know what they say. You should keep your mouth shut and let people think you are a fool, rather than open your mouth and remove all doubt.

ALAN. I'm afraid to talk now.

DANIELLE. Perhaps we're getting somewhere. Are you done with your dinner?

ALAN. Yes. I can't eat right now.

DANIELLE. Well, would you like some apple pie?

ALAN. WHAT?

DANIELLE. Apple pie, Alan. Would you like a piece of apple pie?

ALAN. Why would I want an apple?

DANIELLE. That's odd, Alan. I didn't ask you if you wanted an apple. I asked you if you wanted a slice of apple pie.

ALAN. Why would I want an apple pie today?

DANIELLE. Who doesn't like apple pie? That's what I did after the coffee shop this morning, by the way. I went to the market and you wouldn't believe it if you saw it with your own two eyes. Right there in the produce section

What Do They Become? by Jared Kelner – copyright 2014
jared@jaredkelner.com – www.jaredkelner.com

was this beautiful display of organic apples. They made it look like you were at the orchard. There was grass on the ground, those woven wooden baskets and little children were picking the apples off the fake tree and putting them into their baskets. It was touching and then suddenly I became quite sad, Alan. I hadn't realized it, but this little girl who was with her father came over to me and tapped me on my leg. She said, "Ma'am, why are you crying?" and I looked down at her and said, "Am I?" and she said, "Why yes, Ma'am. You are." And I said, "I don't know why." She walked away with her father, hand in hand, and as I watched her turn into the next aisle, I thought to myself, I do know why I'm crying. And it was not because of your betrayal. I was crying because I felt as if I failed, as a wife. I was crying because I never became a mother. And I realized I was crying because I've never once baked you an apple pie in eighteen years. So I wiped the tears from my eyes and bought the ingredients to bake you the most delicious apple pie you've ever tasted. I came home and I baked, Alan. To the best of my ability, I baked you a pie. So, I'll ask you again, would you like a piece of my apple pie?

ALAN. I love you, Danielle.

What Do They Become? by Jared Kelner – copyright 2014
jared@jaredkelner.com – www.jaredkelner.com

DANIELLE. I'm not there yet, Alan, but I will get there for us and for the sake of the child. Now, would you like a piece of my apple pie?

ALAN. Yes, please.

DANIELLE. Very well. It's there for you on the counter. The blanket is on the couch. I will see you in the morning.

ALAN. Goodnight, Danielle.

DANIELLE. Sleep well, Alan.

(Danielle exits to the bedroom as Alan remains frozen at the table. Lights out)

Scene 5: (Amber and Vinnie's apartment, very late the same day) The lights come up downstage center and we see Amber, wearing pajamas, sitting on the floor on the make-shift bed (the blanket and pillows from the couch). Vinnie enters from upstage right holding a small bottle of bourbon that is almost finished. He is somewhere between drunk and sober.

AMBER. Have you been drinking?

VINNIE. A little.

AMBER. Was it a bad day today, baby?

VINNIE. Don't ask me that, Amber, you know how my day was.

AMBER. I know, baby. Come sit down. Let me make it better.

VINNIE. Amber. Not now. I don't want to be touched.

AMBER. It's not your fault.

VINNIE. Just words, Amber.

AMBER. It's not your fault.

VINNIE. You don't understand.

AMBER. Don't tell me I don't understand. I was there.

VINNIE. Then you know they're just words.

AMBER. It's not your fault.

VINNIE. That doesn't make it any easier.

AMBER. I know, baby. I know today is hard for you. I know how much you blame yourself, but you are not to blame.

VINNIE. He was just a little baby.

AMBER. I know. It's not your fault.

VINNIE. Why did he drown, Amber?

AMBER. You know why, Vinnie.

VINNIE. Cause I left him.

AMBER. No.

VINNIE. Cause I left him, Amber.

What Do They Become? by Jared Kelner – copyright 2014
jared@jaredkelner.com – www.jaredkelner.com

AMBER. Vinnie. You are not to blame. This is not your fault. No five-year-old should ever be responsible for that.

VINNIE. But I left him.

AMBER. Why did you leave him?

VINNIE. They were fighting again.

AMBER. What did he do?

VINNIE. He hit her.

AMBER. Again?

VINNIE. Again.

AMBER. So you ran to protect her.

VINNIE. He was punching her in the eye. I tried to stop him, but I was too small.

AMBER. You were five. You were a baby.

VINNIE. I wasn't the baby.

AMBER. It's not your fault, Vinnie. It was their job to give him a bath.

VINNIE. I tried to protect her.

AMBER. But he hit you.

VINNIE. I fell down next to her.

AMBER. Who was she, Vinnie?

VINNIE. Ma'am.

AMBER. Mom?

What Do They Become? by Jared Kelner – copyright 2014
jared@jaredkelner.com – www.jaredkelner.com

VINNIE. Not mom. Just ma'am.

AMBER. Did she love you?

VINNIE. I don't know.

AMBER. Did she love you, Vinnie?

VINNIE. No.

AMBER. But you loved her?

VINNIE. Yes.

AMBER. Why?

VINNIE. Because I was a baby.

AMBER. And do babies watch babies?

VINNIE. No.

AMBER. So it's not your fault.

VINNIE. It's not my fault.

AMBER. And that animal who only fostered kids for the money? What did he do while you laid on the floor and the baby was in the tub?

VINNIE. He took a beer from the fridge and sat on the couch and watched us cry.

AMBER. And the baby?

VINNIE. There was silence. She knew. She threw me off and ran to the bathroom. She pulled him from the water, but he was gone. She screamed. I feel that scream down my back every day. And he just sat on the couch and did nothing.

AMBER. I watched from my window across the street. I remember the spinning lights. I remember the sirens. I remember the rain. I remember watching you sit on the front porch alone. You just sat there shivering and crying.

VINNIE. I cried.

AMBER. All night. I watched you. They never came to bring you back inside. They left you out there, in the rain, alone. They blamed you, Vinnie, but it was not your fault. It was their fault. They are to blame, not you.

VINNIE. I hate them.

AMBER. You need to hit something? To get it out of you?

VINNIE. I don't know.

AMBER. You need to hit something? Hit me, Vinnie. Hit me. I'll be your punching bag. I'll be ma'am. I'll be him for you. Hit me, Vinnie. Come on. Hit me. Hit me. I can take it. Hit me til it stops hurting.

VINNIE. (Vinnie reaches back to hit Amber, but breaks down before he punches. She catches him and holds him tight). Why do you love me?

AMBER. Don't ask me that. You know why. You know what went on in my house. Those monsters that took me in were no different. You know what he did to his wife and to the other girls that lived with us. You know what he did to me. But it's not about me today. Today is for you.

VINNIE. I saw you watching me from across the street that night.

AMBER. I know.

VINNIE. I've always loved you.

AMBER. I'm here, baby. I am never leaving.

VINNIE. What we do, Amber, what we are doing here to Alan and Danielle and to the others before them, it's important. You know that right?

AMBER. I know, baby.

VINNIE. Why didn't they love us?

AMBER. It's not our fault. But we are fixing it. OK? We are making a difference. (Amber sits behind Vinnie and massages his shoulders)

VINNIE. That feels good.

AMBER. You like that, right?

VINNIE. Yeah.

AMBER. That's what I'm talking about, Officer Johnny. You're one sexy cop.

VINNIE. Shut up, Samantha. You're such a goof. Just massage me.

AMBER. Whatever you say, Officer.

VINNIE. I love you.

AMBER. Whatever.

VINNIE. How did it go today?

AMBER. Um, perfect.

VINNIE. How perfect?

AMBER. Like perfect, perfect.

VINNIE. Exactly how we planned?

AMBER. Better. They have no idea what's coming.

VINNIE. Tell me what happened.

AMBER. Your research was amazing this time.

VINNIE. She believed you.

AMBER. She called me Sam, Samantha like a hundred times. Then, I seduced him again in his office.

VINNIE. Hold on. You got both of them today?

AMBER. So, you were right. She's like clockwork. Every morning at 8:15 she gets her coffee. So I went there at like 8:00 and just sat outside and waited. 8:15 comes and who walks up?

VINNIE. She did?

AMBER. Yep. Sad, exhausted, hungover Danielle.

VINNIE. 8:15 on the dot?

AMBER. On the fucking dot, Vinnie. You're like some kind of surveillance guru.

VINNIE. Awesome.

AMBER. So she's walking out with her coffee and I turn and like fake bump into her and apologize. I'm like, "I'm sorry" and she's like, "Don't worry about it" and I'm like, "Wait, I know you" and she's like, "No" and I'm like, "Um yeah, we've met" and then she fucking recognizes me. I mean her face dropped when she saw who I was.

VINNIE. What did you do?

AMBER. I played along like I couldn't put two and two together, but then it's like, shit, I'm the one from the bathroom.

VINNIE. Then what?

AMBER. Like we expected. She attacked, but I worked her. I told her about Johnny, my hot cop boyfriend.

VINNIE. I liked Johnny. He was a badass.

AMBER. I liked Samantha.

VINNIE. They were good people. So, what next?

AMBER. So I convinced her the whole thing is basically her fault. She told me she hasn't slept with Alan for three months?

VINNIE. Are you fucking kidding me?

What Do They Become? by Jared Kelner – copyright 2014
jared@jaredkelner.com – www.jaredkelner.com

AMBER. No. Unreal, right?

VINNIE. We nailed it this time, Amber.

AMBER. So then I casually mention a threesome and a minute later, she has this fucking epiphany. She thinks she thought it up on her own. She tells me I have to go over to her house tomorrow night to do them both.

VINNIE. You're amazing. This is the smoothest it's ever gone for us. Remember how bad it went in Tempe?

AMBER. Yeah. What about San Jose?

VINNIE. Yeah, that was bad too.

AMBER. But we've gotten better and this one will be great.

VINNIE. Our best yet. Their file had everything. She drinks, the car crash, he embezzles. These people are fucked up, right?

AMBER. Yeah, but there's something different about them. They love each other. They're just lost.

VINNIE. Yeah. I know.

AMBER. Oh, so anyway, after she left, I went to work and seduced Alan in his office. He doesn't know if he's coming or going.

VINNIE. Apparently he's not cumming at all.

AMBER. Ha Ha. Good one.

What Do They Become? by Jared Kelner – copyright 2014
jared@jaredkelner.com – www.jaredkelner.com

VINNIE. Thank you. But you'll fix that tomorrow night.

AMBER. Yes, I will.

VINNIE. Just don't enjoy it too much, ok?

AMBER. I'll be thinking of you. Oh! He called that guy Mike today.

VINNIE. What? Mike from the lawsuit?

AMBER. Yeah, I think so. He was doing something shady.

VINNIE. What's with these people?

AMBER. I don't know.

VINNIE. We gotta work this one hard, baby.

AMBER. I know.

VINNIE. You should go back to the coffee shop tomorrow morning. She's probably going to be having second thoughts, right?

AMBER. Maybe, I guess she could.

VINNIE. Yeah. Go to the coffee shop tomorrow and get her all sexed up again. She's got to leave ready to do something crazy.

AMBER. I'll take care of it.

VINNIE. Then, tomorrow night, we go to their house. Get them into the bedroom, get them naked and make them face the window. I'll snap a few pictures from outside and then when you hear me honk the horn, just grab your shit and get the hell out of there.

AMBER. And then what?

VINNIE. Then we come back here to print the pictures.

AMBER. I frigging love you.

VINNIE. Back at you, Amber.

AMBER. Call me Samantha, would you?

VINNIE. Only if you call me Johnny.

AMBER. OK, Johnny. I love you, Johnny.

VINNIE. And I love you too, Samantha.

(Lights out)

Scene 6: (A coffee shop, the next morning) The lights come up on the coffee shop. Samantha is sitting at the table outside the coffee shop with 2 cups of coffee. Danielle approaches from stage right and before she enters the coffee shop, Samantha stops her.

SAMANTHA. Good morning, lover.

DANIELLE. What? Oh, hi. Good morning.

SAMANTHA. I knew you'd be back. Here, I got you a latte.

(Samantha hands Danielle the coffee)

DANIELLE. Thank you, but why are you here?

SAMANTHA. Well, to see you of course, silly.

DANIELLE. Why do you need to see me?

SAMANTHA. Cause I assumed you were going to be all depressed and shit and having second thoughts all night and like you were thinking about should you really go through with it and about your marriage and about if you still love Alan and blah, blah, blah. Am I right?

DANIELLE. That's literally every thought that was running around in my mind all night.

SAMANTHA. So, that's why I'm here. Sit down and let's talk like girlfriends again, ok?

DANIELLE. OK. (They sit) How did you know what I would be thinking?

SAMANTHA. Because you've never done anything like this before and I knew you'd talk yourself out of it. You probably went home and did some boring housewife shit. Am I right? Well, I'm here to tell you that if you really love Alan, the only way to save your marriage, is to do something crazy.

DANIELLE. That makes sense.

SAMANTHA. I know, right? Like if you tried to do this on your own, what would you do?

What Do They Become? by Jared Kelner – copyright 2014
jared@jaredkelner.com – www.jaredkelner.com

DANIELLE. I don't know. I've never done anything like this before.

SAMANTHA. Exactly, so you're not coming from a place of experience. I am. I know how to do this, Danielle. I don't want to brag, but I'm hot in bed. I mean look at me, right?

DANIELLE. You do look good.

SAMANTHA. It's cause I got the passion inside me. But, back to you. If you had to do this on your own, what would you do?

DANIELLE. I don't know. Perhaps scented candles. Some rose petals. A bubble bath I guess.

SAMANTHA. Danielle, is this a day at the spa for you or do you want to get your husband back? Rule number one, no scented candles. A man wants sex, not potpourri.

DANIELLE. I told you, I don't know what to do here.

SAMANTHA. That's what I'm saying. So you need me, right?

DANIELLE. Right. I need you. You are making so much sense. You're helping to clear my head. I felt so conflicted all night and when I left this morning, I was resigned to cancel the whole thing.

SAMANTHA. And now?

DANIELLE. And now, I want to learn more.

What Do They Become? by Jared Kelner – copyright 2014
jared@jaredkelner.com – www.jaredkelner.com

SAMANTHA. There you go. What do you want to know?

DANIELLE. Well, what should I expect tonight?

SAMANTHA. Don't ever have expectations, Danielle. Expectations are the mother of disappointment.

DANIELLE. Profound.

SAMANTHA. I know, right? I saw that shit on some homeless guy's sign last week. I'm like, "Fuck! That's some deep shit there, homeless dude." And he's like, "Fuck off, gimme a dollar." So I gave that asshole a dollar. You know why?

DANIELLE. Why?

SAMANTHA. Cause he had the balls to go after it. And that's what you need, Danielle. You need homeless guy balls. You need to say, "Fuck it. This shit is happening tonight cause I love my man and he deserves to have his world rocked." Say that, Danielle.

DANIELLE. I could never.

SAMANTHA. You want me to slap you?

DANIELLE. You mean tonight?

SAMANTHA. No, you crazy bitch, I mean now.

DANIELLE. Oh. I can't say that. It's just not natural for me to speak like that.

What Do They Become? by Jared Kelner – copyright 2014
jared@jaredkelner.com – www.jaredkelner.com

SAMANTHA. That's my point. If you can't even say it here with me, what's gonna happen tonight when the three of us are naked in bed together? You're gonna clam up and that can't happen. Am I right?

DANIELLE. You are right. You're like some kind of motivational sex therapist.

SAMANTHA. I know, right?

DANIELLE. OK, let's do this.

SAMANTHA. There you go, Danielle.

DANIELLE. What do I say again?

SAMANTHA. Whatever you want.

DANIELLE. Just get me started.

SAMANTHA. OK. You say, "Fuck it."

DANIELLE. Fuck it.

SAMANTHA. This shit is happening tonight.

DANIELLE. This shit is happening tonight.

SAMANTHA. With more feeling.

DANIELLE. This shit is happening tonight!

SAMANTHA. Good. Cause I love my man.

DANIELLE. Cause I love my man.

SAMANTHA. I don't believe you Danielle.

DANIELLE. Cause I love my man.

SAMANTHA. WHAT?

What Do They Become? by Jared Kelner – copyright 2014
jared@jaredkelner.com – www.jaredkelner.com

DANIELLE. CAUSE I LOVE MY MAN!

SAMANTHA. AND HE DESERVES TO HAVE HIS WORLD ROCKED!

DANIELLE. AND HE DESERVES TO HAVE HIS WORLD ROCKED!

SAMANTHA. How do you feel?

DANIELLE. I feel hot.

SAMANTHA. You look hot.

DANIELLE. You look hot.

SAMANTHA. I know, right? Look at me. I'm hot. You're hot. We are two hot chicks and we're gonna tear Alan apart.

DANIELLE. We're gonna rock his world.

SAMANTHA. That's right, Danielle, now you go home and get ready for tonight. You get all sexy and shit. Put on some slutty clothes and some apple red lipstick and whatever you do, no panties, you got it?

DANIELLE. No panties?

SAMANTHA. No panties.

DANIELLE. Ooh, I like that. Should I take them off here?

SAMANTHA. No, Danielle. You want to get arrested?

DANIELLE. I love it.

SAMANTHA. Come here. Give me a hug.

What Do They Become? by Jared Kelner – copyright 2014
jared@jaredkelner.com – www.jaredkelner.com

DANIELLE. (They stand and hug) Thank you, Sam.

SAMANTHA. This means more to me than you know, Danielle. I can't wait for tonight.

DANIELLE. 7:00. Don't be late.

SAMANTHA. I'll be there. Now go home and get ready for a night that will change your lives forever. (As Danielle turns to leave, Samantha slaps her ass. Danielle runs off all sexed up)

(Lights out)

Scene 7: (A park bench, around 6 PM the same day) The lights come up with a blue moonlight feel downstage center. Alan is sitting alone on a park bench (the coffee table from the house, simply pulled downstage) with 2 handled shopping bags next to him. Vinnie, in his police uniform, watches Alan for a moment and then approaches from stage left.

JOHNNY. Everything alright tonight, sir?

ALAN. What? Yeah. I'm ok.

JOHNNY. Are you sure about that?

ALAN. Yeah. I mean, I guess. I don't know.

JOHNNY. Wife troubles?

ALAN. Is it that obvious?

JOHNNY. Just part of the job. You know, we see this kind of thing a lot. A man sitting alone on a bench, at night, after work, in deep thought. It's either gonna be the wife or the kids. I pegged you for wife troubles.

ALAN. You're good at what you do.

JOHNNY. You have no idea.

ALAN. I'll be alright. I hope. I screwed up.

JOHNNY. What did you do?

ALAN. You know.

JOHNNY. You hit her?

ALAN. No. God no.

JOHNNY. Good. I don't put up with that. You beat your wife, you deserve to get your ass kicked by someone like me. You cheated, huh? You got caught.

ALAN. I didn't really get caught. Well, no that's not true. She saw us. I kissed her. Maybe a little more, too.

JOHNNY. Excuse me?!

ALAN. What?

JOHNNY. What do you mean, "Maybe a little more"?

ALAN. Wait. I'm sorry. This is a personal issue. I've got it under control.

JOHNNY. So you cheated, huh? And you think it'll just disappear? Like it never happened and there won't be consequences?

ALAN. No. It's not like that at all.

JOHNNY. No?

ALAN. No. I owned up to it, mostly. I don't want to hurt her any more. So, as far as she knows, it was just a kiss. She's pissed and I deserve it.

JOHNNY. Alright then.

ALAN. Look, I'm just going through a rough patch.

JOHNNY. Is that right? Your kids giving you trouble too?

ALAN. No. We don't have kids.

JOHNNY. No kids? Really?

ALAN. No. Not yet. Soon, maybe. Hopefully.

JOHNNY. Yeah? Is that right? You want kids?

ALAN. Yes.

JOHNNY. That's a big step, right?

ALAN. Very big.

JOHNNY. Don't I know it.

ALAN. Oh, yeah? You have kids?

JOHNNY. Me? No. No kids. None of my own, at least. Not married. Hot girlfriend, though. You'd like her.

ALAN. What do you mean, "It's a big step" then?

What Do They Become? by Jared Kelner – copyright 2014
jared@jaredkelner.com – www.jaredkelner.com

JOHNNY. Well, you know. I've seen things firsthand. So-called parents. Marital problems. Drugs. Neglect. Abuse. Betrayal. Abandonment. Broken systems. Kids basically raising themselves. Learning how to survive in the streets. You know. I've seen things.

ALAN. That's sad.

JOHNNY. For who?

ALAN. I guess the kids, mostly.

JOHNNY. Not mostly, pal. It's always about the kids. What do you think happens to some of these kids when the parents are total fuck-ups? Huh? You think everything just magically turns out ok for them?

ALAN. No, I'm not saying that.

JOHNNY. Then what are you saying?

ALAN. Just that I get it.

JOHNNY. Do you?

ALAN. Yes. My wife and I are going to become foster parents for that exact reason.

JOHNNY. And what reason is that?

ALAN. To help. To be there for them.

JOHNNY. But you cheated?

ALAN. I know.

JOHNNY. What kind of a father does that?

ALAN. I wasn't thinking.

JOHNNY. Is that what you told your wife?

ALAN. Look, I'm getting uncomfortable with this conversation.

JOHNNY. Can't take the heat. I get it. You're a lightweight.

ALAN. Excuse me?

JOHNNY. Just calling it like I see it, pal.

ALAN. Hey. I'm trying to make it right. I love my wife.

JOHNNY. Then what are you doing here sitting on a bench talking to me?

ALAN. I'm not.

JOHNNY. Good. Go home.

ALAN. Goodnight, officer. (Alan leaves. Vinnie sheds the Johnny persona and becomes himself)

VINNIE. Goodnight, Alan. (Vinnie calls Amber on his cellphone. Spotlight shines on Amber getting dressed in their apartment) Hey, you ready?

AMBER. I'm getting dressed. Where are you?

VINNIE. I was tailing Alan after he left work.

AMBER. What? Why?

VINNIE. Just making sure we're set.

AMBER. And?

What Do They Become? by Jared Kelner – copyright 2014
jared@jaredkelner.com – www.jaredkelner.com

VINNIE. And the guy's struggling.

AMBER. What do you mean? What did he do?

VINNIE. It's not what he did. It's what he said.

AMBER. You talked to him?

VINNIE. Yeah.

AMBER. Why would you do that?

VINNIE. Cause he was driving all over town and he ended up sitting on a bench.

AMBER. Who did you say you were?

VINNIE. I'm in uniform. He didn't ask.

AMBER. So what did he say?

VINNIE. He said he kissed you.

AMBER. You knew that already.

VINNIE. Then he said you did more than kiss.

AMBER. Babe, you know I'm just working him, right?

VINNIE. Yeah, but when he said it, I almost smacked him.

AMBER. You didn't touch him did you?

VINNIE. No. Of course not.

AMBER. Good, cause you gotta keep your head.

VINNIE. I know. Look, forget it. Just get ready. I'll be home in ten minutes.

AMBER. I'll be ready.

(They hang up and the lights fade out)

What Do They Become? by Jared Kelner – copyright 2014
jared@jaredkelner.com – www.jaredkelner.com

Scene 8: (Alan and Danielle's house, just before 7 PM the same day) The lights come up full on the house. Danielle is pacing in the room and is anxiously waiting for Alan to come home. She is drinking a glass of white wine and taking big gulps as she waits. She is wearing a robe that is covering her sexy outfit. Scented candles are placed around the room. Alan enters carrying 2 large shopping bags.

DANIELLE. Where have you been? It's almost 7:00. (Alan does not answer. He just stands by the door taking the room in) Alan. Where were you? You got off work at five.
ALAN. What's with the candles?
DANIELLE. Never mind that. Did you go shopping?
ALAN. Danielle, could you sit down for a minute?
DANIELLE. Why?
ALAN. Please, just sit down. I've been doing a lot of thinking and I've got a lot to say, so please, just sit down. (She sits on the couch). Is that cinnamon?
DANIELLE. What's going on, Alan?
ALAN. (He sits on the couch next to Danielle and puts the bags on the floor in front of him) OK. Danielle. First, please forgive me. It was wrong what I did. You are the love of

my life and I put our marriage and the chance to finally be parents in jeopardy.

DANIELLE. Well, Alan, let's not get carried away. It was just one kiss after all.

ALAN. What?

DANIELLE. She's an attractive woman and I know that things for us have been a little...infrequent lately.

ALAN. Huh?

DANIELLE. All I'm saying, Alan, is that I understand why you did it. We've made an important decision to bring a child into our lives and I appreciate how stressful that could be after all these years.

ALAN. It was still wrong to kiss her, right?

DANIELLE. Yes. It was, Alan. It was wrong, but I understand.

ALAN. This is not the conversation I was expecting to have tonight.

DANIELLE. Well, you know what they say, "expectation is the mother of disappointment."

ALAN. That's a good one.

DANIELLE. I know, right? So, what's with the bags?

ALAN. Well, I feel foolish now.

DANIELLE. Were you going to woo me, Alan?

ALAN. Kind of.

DANIELLE. Oh Yay!!! This is so exciting. OK. Woo me, Alan. I'm ready to be wooed.

ALAN. Seriously?

DANIELLE. Woo away.

ALAN. OK. (Reaching into his bag, he takes out one yellow rose) On day one, I knocked on your door and your father answered. He said, "Is that for me?" and I said, "No, sir, it's for your daughter." As you walked down the stairs, my heart stopped for a moment. You looked beautiful for our first date. I gave you a yellow rose like this one and said…

DANIELLE. "Hey, Dannie, you look beautiful."

ALAN. You remember?

DANIELLE. I remember.

ALAN. And you still look beautiful today. (He reaches into his bag and pulls out a box of corn flakes) Day one hundred fifty-one. You spent the night for the first time. My friends were teasing me that we were never going to "do it", but I didn't care when it happened. I just wanted to hold you. When we made love for the first time, it was clumsy, but beautiful. And afterwards, you said, "I'm hungry, got any corn flakes?" So, I ran downstairs and brought you up a big bowl of cereal. You sat up in my bed and ate and we talked all night. (He reaches into his bag and pulls out a bowtie) Day 1,040, was our wedding. I was so nervous. I threw up.

DANIELLE. I smelled it on your breath.

ALAN. But you kissed me anyway.

DANIELLE. But I kissed you anyway.

ALAN. And again, I knew you loved me and I made a vow to always love you. And these last few months, I lost sight of that. (He reaches into his bag and pulls out a surgical mask) Day 1,204. That's the day of the accident. You drank too much. I should have never let you drive. When the car finally stopped, my leg was shattered and you didn't wake up. I thought I lost you. They rushed us to the hospital and brought you into surgery. I was crumbling inside, but tried to hold it together. They told me we would never have children of our own and I said, as long as I still had you, that would be enough. And you pulled through like the amazing woman you are.

DANIELLE. (She hugs him tightly) I love you, Alan.

ALAN. I love you so much. I have more in the bag.

DANIELLE. Keep going. (The doorbell rings) OH, FUCK!

ALAN. What?

What Do They Become? by Jared Kelner – copyright 2014
jared@jaredkelner.com – www.jaredkelner.com

DANIELLE. Um. Oh shit, it's seven. Um. OK, Alan. Look, I love you. Just know that we are going to be fine. (Doorbell rings again) Oh fuck, oh fuck oh fuck.

ALAN. What's going on?

DANIELLE. Um, just answer the door. (Alan goes to the door, which is offstage)

SAMANTHA. (Offstage) Hi, Alan.

ALAN. (Offstage) WHAT THE FUCK!

DANIELLE. Who is it, sweetheart?

ALAN. (Alan poking his head back onstage, to Danielle) Um, nobody, honey. (Alan now back offstage, to Samantha) What are you doing here? How do you know where I live?

DANIELLE. Honey, who is it?

ALAN. (Alan poking his head back onstage, to Danielle) Nobody. I'll be right there. (Alan goes offstage again. Danielle puts on lipstick and high heels)

SAMANTHA. (Offstage) So are you gonna let me in, stud?

ALAN. (Offstage) What? Why?

SAMANTHA. (Offstage) Oh, Alan, you're adorable. Get out of my way. I'm coming in. (Samantha pushes Alan aside, enters, and walks right up to Danielle downstage center.

They stare at each other for a moment. Alan crosses downstage left of Samantha)

DANIELLE. Hello, Samantha.

SAMANTHA. Hello, Danielle. (Danielle tosses her robe to the couch revealing her sexy outfit) DAMN! You look hot.

DANIELLE. You look hot.

SAMANTHA. Are we good to go?

DANIELLE. We're good to go.

SAMANTHA. Good.

ALAN. WHAT IS GOING ON HERE? (To Danielle) WHAT ARE YOU WEARING?

DANIELLE. Alan, sit down and catch your breath.

ALAN. What? Why? Why am I sitting down? (To Samantha) What are you doing here? (To Danielle) What is she doing here?

DANIELLE. Alan, just breathe. Sit down.

SAMANTHA. Yeah, Alan, just sit down and take a deep long breath. (Samantha takes Alan's hand and sits down on the couch next to him) Loosen up. Relax. You're all backed up. (Danielle sits next to Alan as Samantha rubs his thigh)

ALAN. Um, ok.

DANIELLE. Sweetie, as you can see, Samantha is here.

SAMANTHA. Hi, honey.

DANIELLE. I've invited Samantha here to help us.

ALAN. Help us? How could she possibly help us?

SAMANTHA. Oh Alan, you're so silly. You always make me laugh.

DANIELLE. You see, Alan. Samantha and I have become, well...girlfriends.

SAMANTHA. Awww.

ALAN. WHAT? WHEN? HOW?

DANIELLE. It doesn't really matter, but at the coffee shop.

ALAN. What?

DANIELLE. Breathe, Alan. Breathe. So, Samantha and I got to talking and she's quite bright.

SAMANTHA. See Alan, I told you I was smart.

DANIELLE. And she got me thinking that the whole ninety-four days had a lot to do with me never being in the mood. There are aspects to the situation that you are responsible for, but it's complicated and irrelevant right now. So, as we talked, I decided the best way to snap us out of our rut was to do something crazy, so...here she is.

SAMANTHA. Here I am, Alan.

ALAN. I don't understand.

What Do They Become? by Jared Kelner – copyright 2014
jared@jaredkelner.com – www.jaredkelner.com

DANIELLE. Alan, I love you, but like Sam said, you're backed up, and tonight, we are going to help you relieve your tension.

ALAN. We? What do you mean, "We?"

SAMANTHA. Both of us, Alan. Come on. Get with it. Your wife is hot. I'm hot. The three of us. In there, (pointing to the bedroom) doing stuff you know you've been thinking about doing.

ALAN. I haven't been thinking about anything.

DANIELLE. Now, Alan. It's ok. This is my gift to you. To us. To rekindle our passion.

SAMANTHA. (To Danielle) Speaking of kindling, I said no candles.

DANIELLE. I know, I'm sorry.

SAMANTHA. It's ok. You'll learn.

DANIELLE. So, Alan, this is going to happen.

ALAN. Seriously?

DANIELLE. Seriously.

SAMANTHA. Seriously.

ALAN. And this is what you want?

DANIELLE. Yes, Alan. I want you. I want Samantha. I want you to want me. I want you to want Samantha. I want us all to want each other all night long.

What Do They Become? by Jared Kelner – copyright 2014
jared@jaredkelner.com – www.jaredkelner.com

ALAN. You're the best wife ever!

DANIELLE. I know, right?

ALAN. So, how does this work?

DANIELLE. I don't know. Don't look at me. This is my first time too.

SAMANTHA. Oh, you two are adorable. Come with me. (Samantha grabs both their hands and pulls them both into the bedroom downstage left. Moments later, the lights come down on the house and a single spotlight comes up downstage center as Vinnie enters and faces the audience as if he's outside the house looking through the window. Vinnie takes 3 pictures and we see 3 flashes. He sprints off stage. Moments later we hear a car horn honk. Then moments later we hear a car peeling out and screeching away)

(Lights out)

Scene 9: (A coffee shop, the next morning) Lights come up on the coffee shop. Vinnie, wearing a police officer's uniform and Amber, in comfortable clothes, sit at the outside table looking at the pictures Vinnie took last night and plan the next step.

What Do They Become? by Jared Kelner – copyright 2014
jared@jaredkelner.com – www.jaredkelner.com

VINNIE. These pictures are perfect. You did amazing last night.

AMBER. You too, baby. So, what now?

VINNIE. So now, I take care of her. You take care of him. We meet at the bus stop and move on to the next one.

AMBER. What do you think will happen to them?

VINNIE. I don't know.

AMBER. I hope they make the right decision.

VINNIE. Me too. They're not like the others. They could be good parents if they try, but you never know. And if they don't go through with it, it's for the better, cause the kid would get dumped back into the system. And then he'd end up like us.

AMBER. What about us, Vinnie? Are we gonna make it?

VINNIE. Amber, look, you know I love you. But it's not about us right now.

AMBER. I know, but when's it gonna be our time?

VINNIE. I don't know, but it's not now.

AMBER. It's never gonna be the right time. We're never gonna be done. There's always gonna be another kid.

VINNIE. You think I don't know that?

AMBER. I'm just saying, we deserve some happiness, that's all.

What Do They Become? by Jared Kelner – copyright 2014
jared@jaredkelner.com – www.jaredkelner.com

VINNIE. You're not happy?

AMBER. I'm not talking about being happy. I'm talking about happiness. I'm talking about a future where we can breathe without choking. Look, I get it. I do. I just want to love you. That's all.

VINNIE. So love me. I know you want the fairytale, but that's never going to be us. You have to know that and you have to be ok with that.

AMBER. I know. I am.

VINNIE. Alright then. Are we good?

AMBER. Of course, baby.

VINNIE. Good. Give me a kiss. (She kisses gently) OK, it's almost 8:15. She'll be here any minute. You gotta get out of here now. (Vinnie hands her a manila envelope with pictures) Take these and go to the office. Do your thing and I'll see you in an hour. The bus leaves at 10:00. Don't be late.

AMBER. I love you.

VINNIE. I love you, too. (Amber leaves. Vinnie gets up and stands by the coffee shop door. Moments later, Danielle approaches. She's in a fog and sits down at the outside table. Vinnie approaches holding an envelope)

JOHNNY. Excuse me, ma'am?

What Do They Become? by Jared Kelner – copyright 2014
jared@jaredkelner.com – www.jaredkelner.com

DANIELLE. (Danielle looks up and sees the police officer). Yes? Good morning, officer. Is everything alright?

JOHNNY. You're Danielle Miller, correct?

DANIELLE. Yes. Why? Did something happen?

JOHNNY. That's up to you, ma'am.

DANIELLE. I'm sorry. I don't follow.

JOHNNY. You and your husband. You filed papers with the state, correct? To become foster parents? Is that right?

DANIELLE. Yes, yes we have. I'm sorry. Why are you here?

JOHNNY. Do you believe you and Alan should be doing this?

DANIELLE. Excuse me?

JOHNNY. It's a simple question. Are you and Alan ready to become parents?

DANIELLE. I'm sorry. I didn't catch your name?

JOHNNY. It's Officer Johnny Rollins. I believe you know my girlfriend, Samantha.

DANIELLE. What about Samantha?

JOHNNY. Yes. What's going on with you and Samantha?

DANIELLE. Nothing. Why? You're Samantha's boyfriend?

JOHNNY. Yes, ma'am.

DANIELLE. But why are you here? What happened?

What Do They Become? by Jared Kelner – copyright 2014
jared@jaredkelner.com – www.jaredkelner.com

JOHNNY. Nothing yet, ma'am. I'll ask you one more time. Do you believe you and Alan are ready to be parents?

DANIELLE. I am not comfortable with this conversation.

JOHNNY. You seemed very comfortable last night.

DANIELLE. EXCUSE ME!!!

JOHNNY. Danielle. This is not about you, so settle down. This is about the child.

DANIELLE. What about the child?

JOHNNY. I'd hate for these pictures to end up with Child Services. It would be a shame if your case worker saw these. (Danielle grabs the pictures) I'm not sure your home is a suitable environment for impressionable young children.

DANIELLE. Oh my god!!! Where did you get these? Who took these pictures? Who are you?

JOHNNY. I told you, Danielle. I'm Officer Johnny Rollins. I'm Samantha's boyfriend.

DANIELLE. I heard you. What do you want? Why are you doing this?

JOHNNY. I'm not doing anything, Danielle. I was not the one in bed with another woman last night and I'm not the one who smells like alcohol at eight in the morning.

DANIELLE. How dare you! Did you take these, you pervert? Were you at my house? What is your badge number?

JOHNNY. That's not the question you should be asking.

DANIELLE. Is that right?

JOHNNY. Yes, that's right.

DANIELLE. What do you want?

JOHNNY. I already asked you.

DANIELLE. What do you want?

JOHNNY. Are you ready?

DANIELLE. What do you care? How is that any of your business?

JOHNNY. Danielle, answer the fucking question. Are you and Alan ready to love someone else's child?

DANIELLE. I don't know.

JOHNNY. And if you don't like the child you get? What then? You just call them up and say, "Take it back?" Is that the plan?

DANIELLE. I don't know.

JOHNNY. Well you better know. You better get that shit figured out long before any child ever steps foot into that house. You hear me?

DANIELLE. Yes.

What Do They Become? by Jared Kelner – copyright 2014
jared@jaredkelner.com – www.jaredkelner.com

JOHNNY. You keep those pictures. I have copies.

DANIELLE. Why are you doing this?

JOHNNY. You better get over to Alan's office. Samantha is having the same talk with him.

DANIELLE. Why?

JOHNNY. Cause you can fuck those kids up for life if you're not ready. Do you understand me?

DANIELLE. I think so.

JOHNNY. Good. We'll be watching you. Now, get out of here. (Danielle runs off. Vinnie sits down at the table) (Lights out)

Scene 10: (Alan's office, around 9 AM the same day) The lights come up on the office. Alan is pacing in his office and Amber enters.

ALAN. What happened last night? Where did you go?

AMBER. I don't have much time, Alan.

ALAN. What are you talking about?

AMBER. Alan, there are things at play here that you don't understand.

ALAN. That's what I'm saying. I don't get what's going on. Where did you go last night?

What Do They Become? by Jared Kelner – copyright 2014
jared@jaredkelner.com – www.jaredkelner.com

AMBER. I left, Alan.

ALAN. I know, but why?

AMBER. Alan, take a breath and calm down.

ALAN. Excuse me?

AMBER. You heard me. Take a breath. You're gonna give yourself a heart attack. Do you wanna die before you even get that child?

ALAN. What? How do you know about that?

AMBER. Alan, you and Danielle are good people. We genuinely like you both.

ALAN. What are you talking about?

AMBER. Do you love your wife?

ALAN. Where did you go last night?

AMBER. ALAN!!! Focus here. Do you love your wife?

ALAN. Yes, of course I love her.

AMBER. Then why would you bring another woman into your bed?

ALAN. Isn't that what she wanted?

AMBER. Maybe, but what did you want? Did you want to cheat on your wife, again, with me, twice?

ALAN. I don't understand.

AMBER. Alan, this is not rocket science. If you love your wife, why would you let me into your bed?

What Do They Become? by Jared Kelner – copyright 2014
jared@jaredkelner.com – www.jaredkelner.com

ALAN. I don't know. Isn't that what you both wanted?

AMBER. What I wanted, Alan, was to find out if you and Danielle were ready.

ALAN. Ready for what?

AMBER. Why are you making this so hard?

ALAN. Ready for what? Samantha, I don't understand.

AMBER. Alan, if you can't figure out how to be a husband, how are you going to be a father?

ALAN. What does one have to do with the other?

AMBER. That's the saddest thing I've heard you say, Alan.

ALAN. Wait a minute. How do you even know that Danielle and I are thinking about that?

AMBER. Thinking about it? What's there to think about? Either you want a child or you don't. There's nothing to think about, Alan. If you don't know whether or not you want to be a father, then you know.

ALAN. Where did you go last night?

AMBER. I went home, Alan.

ALAN. Why?

AMBER. Look, I can't go around and around like this all day. I've got places to be. Take these. (Amber hands the pictures to Alan)

ALAN. What is this? (Alan looks at the pictures) You took these? Are you blackmailing me? Who the fuck are you?

AMBER. Watch it, Alan. If you step out of line, I will email those pictures to Human Resources and tell them you said the only way I was getting David's job is if I slept with you and your wife. They'd fire your ass so fast and when your case worker finds out you got fired for sexual harassment, there's no way they'd ever place a kid with you.

ALAN. Why would you do that?

AMBER. Why would you take being a parent so lightly?

ALAN. We're not.

AMBER. What do you mean?

ALAN. We've been thinking about it for eighteen years.

AMBER. And?

ALAN. And what?

AMBER. And why now?

ALAN. Because we're ready. Because it's something that should be done. If not us, who loves those children? What happens to them? What do they become?

AMBER. Me.

ALAN. What?

What Do They Become? by Jared Kelner – copyright 2014
jared@jaredkelner.com – www.jaredkelner.com

AMBER. Nothing. You're a good man. Goodbye, Alan
(Danielle enters and just as Amber turns to leave, the two women end up standing right in front of each other. They stare at each other for an extended pause without speaking, but saying a lot. Finally, Amber pushes past Danielle and leaves)

ALAN. What are you doing here?

DANIELLE. (Pointing to the pictures) She gave you those?

ALAN. Yes.

DANIELLE. (Showing Alan her pictures) I've got copies, too.

ALAN. How?

DANIELLE. Her boyfriend found me this morning.

ALAN. Boyfriend?

DANIELLE. He's a cop.

ALAN. A cop? What happened?

DANIELLE. He talked to me at the coffee shop and gave me the pictures.

ALAN. What did he want? Was it about last night?

DANIELLE. No. It was about if you and I were ready to be parents.

ALAN. Wait. What?

DANIELLE. He kept asking me if we were ready to foster.

ALAN. That's exactly what she asked me.

What Do They Become? by Jared Kelner – copyright 2014
jared@jaredkelner.com – www.jaredkelner.com

DANIELLE. Why?

ALAN. I don't know. She seemed…damaged, somehow.

DANIELLE. Yeah. Her boyfriend too. Damaged.

ALAN. Something is not right here, Danielle.

DANIELLE. I know, Alan.

ALAN. What should we do now?

DANIELLE. I think we're supposed to talk.

ALAN. About what?

DANIELLE. Us. The baby.

(Lights out)

Scene 11: (A bus stop, around 10 AM the same day)

Lights come up downstage center. Vinnie, now in comfortable travel clothes, is waiting with a duffle bag and a folder of their next target. Amber runs in from stage right.

VINNIE. Amber! Over here.

AMBER. How did it go?

VINNIE. Good. I scared the shit out of her.

AMBER. Alan's head was spinning. I saw Danielle at his office.

VINNIE. And?

What Do They Become? by Jared Kelner – copyright 2014
jared@jaredkelner.com – www.jaredkelner.com

AMBER. And you messed her up pretty bad.

VINNIE. We did good work, Amber.

AMBER. I hope they do it.

VINNIE. I think they will. It'll take time, but under all their insanity, they love each other.

AMBER. Yeah. You know, we're like guardian angels for these kids, Vinnie. I know that what we do is insane, but that's the eighth baby we helped and that means something, right?

VINNIE. Yeah.

AMBER. We're making a difference. We honor his memory every time we do this.

VINNIE. I know, Amber.

AMBER. Good. Cause we can't forget what happened to him. What happened to us. What we've become.

VINNIE. I know.

AMBER. So, where are we off to next?

VINNIE. Atlanta. Here (Vinnie hands Amber a folder), I hacked the Child Services site again last night.

AMBER. Mac and Julie Sutter. What's wrong with them?

VINNIE. He hit her. I have to get more on her when we get down there.

AMBER. What's the angle this time?

What Do They Become? by Jared Kelner – copyright 2014
jared@jaredkelner.com – www.jaredkelner.com

VINNIE. I'll tell you on the bus. It's time to go.

AMBER. (Trying to speak and behave like Danielle) I guess I'm Danielle now. We can put Samantha to bed.

VINNIE. (Trying to speak and behave like Alan) OK, Danielle. You know, I've always wanted to be an Alan.

AMBER. (Trying to speak and behave like Danielle) You look like an Alan.

VINNIE. (Trying to speak and behave like Alan) And you look like a Danielle.

AMBER. (Trying to speak and behave like Danielle) Mac and Julie, watch out. Here comes Alan and Danielle.

(Lights out)

The End.

COSTUMES

Scene 1
Alan: jacket, business casual outfit with tie
Danielle: party dress, low heels
Scene 2
Amber: youthful but sexy business outfit
Danielle: comfortable clothes, scarf
Scene 3
Alan: business casual outfit
Samantha: same as Scene 2, youthful but sexy business outfit
Scene 4
Alan: jacket and same as Scene 3, business casual outfit
Danielle: comfortable clothes
Scene 5
Amber: sweatpants and hoodie
Vinnie: jeans, t-shirt
Scene 6
Samantha: youthful but sexy business outfit.
Danielle: comfortable clothes, scarf
Scene 7
Alan: jacket, business casual outfit
Johnny: police officer uniform
Amber: sexy and revealing outfit
Scene 8
Alan: same as Scene 7 jacket, business casual outfit
Danielle: long robe covering classy but sexy lingerie, high heels
Samantha: same as Scene 7, sexy and revealing outfit
Scene 9
Vinnie: police officer uniform
Amber: comfortable travel clothes
Danielle: comfortable clothes
Scene 10
Alan: business casual outfit
Amber: same as Scene 9, comfortable travel clothes
Danielle: same as Scene 9, comfortable clothes
Scene 11
Vinnie: comfortable travel clothes
Amber: same as Scene 9 comfortable travel clothes, scarf

What Do They Become? by Jared Kelner – copyright 2014
jared@jaredkelner.com – www.jaredkelner.com

What Do They Become? by Jared Kelner – copyright 2014
jared@jaredkelner.com – www.jaredkelner.com

PROPS LIST

Scene 1
Alan: keys
Danielle: purse, vodka bottle, glass
Scene 2
Amber: cellphone, purse
Danielle: purse, sunglasses, coffee cup, pen, notepad
Scene 3
Alan: cellphone, notebook, folder, papers, pen, full pen/pencil holder, apple, wallet, $20 bill
Samantha: No props
Scene 4
Alan: briefcase, keys
Danielle: 2 plates, 2 napkins, 2 forks, 2 knives, 2 glasses, 1 wine glass, 1 bottle of wine, food on 1 plate
Scene 5
Amber: No props
Vinnie: small empty bottle of whiskey
Scene 6
Samantha: 2 cups of coffee, purse
Danielle: purse
Scene 7
Alan: 2 shopping bags, yellow rose, box of corn flakes, bow tie, surgical mask
Johnny: cellphone
Amber: cellphone
Scene 8
Alan: 2 shopping bags, yellow rose, box of corn flakes, bow tie, surgical mask
Danielle: 2 no-flame scented candles, purse, lipstick, compact mirror
Samantha: No props
Scene 9
Vinnie: watch, 2 manila folders with 3 pictures inside each
Amber: backpack
Danielle: purse, small bottle of pills
Scene 10
Alan: notebook, folder, papers, pen, full pen/pencil holder
Amber: backpack, manila folder with 3 pictures inside
Danielle: manila folder with 3 pictures inside
Scene 11
Vinnie: duffle bag, folder with 1 piece of paper inside
Amber: backpack, Danielle's scarf

What Do They Become? by Jared Kelner – copyright 2014
jared@jaredkelner.com – www.jaredkelner.com

What Do They Become? by Jared Kelner – copyright 2014
jared@jaredkelner.com – www.jaredkelner.com

SET LIST

couch, blanket, 2 pillows, coffee table, kitchen table,
2 chairs, side table, desk, 2 chairs

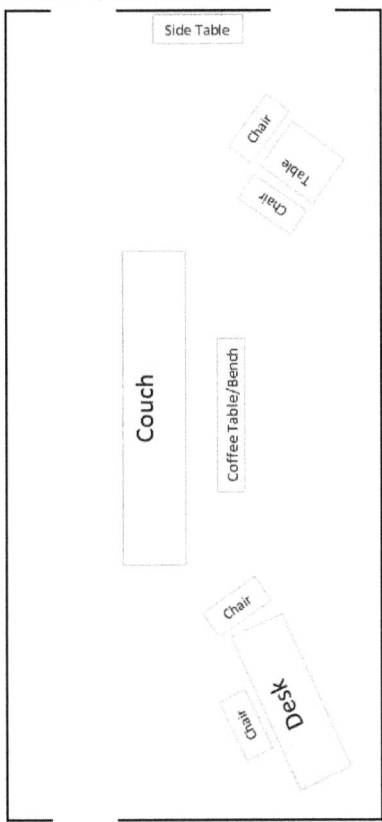

What Do They Become? by Jared Kelner – copyright 2014
jared@jaredkelner.com – www.jaredkelner.com

SOUND CUES

Prior to Lights up for Scene 1
Page 17: ORIGINAL OPENING MUSIC. Fade out as Alan and Danielle enter

Scene 8
Page 76: DOORBELL after Danielle's line "Keep going."
Page 77: 2nd DOORBELL after Danielle's line "Um. Oh shit, it's seven. Um. OK, Alan. Look, I love you. Just know that we are going to be fine."
Page 81: CAR HORN HONK five seconds after Vinnie exits after having taken his 3 pictures
Page 81: CAR PEELING OUT 5 seconds after the car horn honk

Scene 11
Page 94: ORIGINAL CLOSING MUSIC after Amber's line "Here comes Alan and Danielle."

Curtain Call
Same ORIGINAL CLOSING MUSIC continues to play for curtain call.

Contact Jared Kelner at jared@jaredkelner.com to access the original music and audio files for all sound cues.

What Do They Become? by Jared Kelner – copyright 2014
jared@jaredkelner.com – www.jaredkelner.com

LIGHTING DESIGN & CUES

Scene 1
Full stage lights up for start and down for close of scene
Scene 2
Downstage left lights up for start and down for close of scene
Scene 3
Downstage right lights up for start and down for close of scene
Scene 4
Full stage lights up for start and down for close of scene
Scene 5
Downstage center lights up for start and down for close of scene
Scene 6
Downstage left lights up for start and down for close of scene
Scene 7
Downstage center evening color lights up for start of scene. Downstage left lights up on Page 71 after Vinnie's line "Hey, you ready?"
Both lights down for close of scene
Scene 8
Full stage lights up for start and down for close of scene
Scene 9
Downstage left lights up for start and down for close of scene
Scene 10
Downstage right lights up for start and down for close
Scene 11
Downstage center lights up for start and down for close of scene
Curtain Call
Full stage lights up for start and down for close of show

What Do They Become? by Jared Kelner – copyright 2014
jared@jaredkelner.com – www.jaredkelner.com

What Do They Become? by Jared Kelner – copyright 2014
jared@jaredkelner.com – www.jaredkelner.com

What Do They Become?

Written by Jared Kelner

Directed by Gerry Appel

2015 Venus/Adonis Theater Festival
The Robert Moss Theater at 440 Studios
440 Lafayette Street, 3rd Floor, New York, NY 10003

> January 6, 2015 at 9:00 PM
> January 7, 2015 at 6:15 PM
> January 10, 2015 at 7:00 PM

What Do They Become? by Jared Kelner – copyright 2014
jared@jaredkelner.com – www.jaredkelner.com

What Do They Become? by Jared Kelner – copyright 2014
jared@jaredkelner.com – www.jaredkelner.com

For Performance Inquires

Contact Jared Kelner

jared@jaredkelner.com

To watch a video of the

original cast performance, visit

www.jaredkelner.com/Pages/whatdotheybecome.aspx

What Do They Become? by Jared Kelner – copyright 2014
jared@jaredkelner.com – www.jaredkelner.com

www.ingramcontent.com/pod-product-compliance
Lightning Source LLC
Chambersburg PA
CBHW071305040426
42444CB00009B/1871